Bouncing Back From Redundancy

12 Steps to Get Your Career and Life Back on Track

Clive Lewis OBE

A Globis Mediation Group Publication

First published in 2011

By

Globis Mediation Group
Unit 1
Wheatstone Court
Waterwells Business Park
Quedgeley
Gloucester
GL2 2AQ

ISBN 978-0-9568648-5-7

Cover design by Brendan Vaughan-Spruce

Printed and bound in the UK by

Good News Digital Books
23-25 Gunnels Wood Park
Gunnels Wood Road
Stevenage
Hertfordshire
SG1 2BH

Also by Clive Lewis OBE

The Definitive Guide to Workplace Mediation & Managing Conflict at Work

Win Win: Resolving Workplace Conflict: 12 Stories

Difficult Conversations - 10 Steps to Becoming a Tackler not a Dodger

Acknowledgements

I am very grateful to the people who have written about their life experiences of being made redundant for this book. The case studies you are about to read add great richness. I imagine that asking the writers to retell their experiences would not have always brought back memories they would want to relive. This book would be far less appealing without these real life experiences.

I am also thankful to my colleague Philomena for the countless hours spent project managing the publication of the book and to Helen and Tim for their continued proof reading and constant checking of the manuscript. Their efforts have made this book worthy to go into print.

I would also like to thank Brendan Clements who was a test manuscript reader and provided many valuable insights based on his own experiences.

Finally, I am continually grateful to my family who regularly put up with the distraction that comes with writing a book. For their patience, I owe a great deal.

Clive Lewis OBE

Index

Introduction

Being made redundant is a very personal thing. Even if you are one of an entire department that has been let go, the feeling of being surplus to requirements and not being needed will inevitably surface at some point. Very few of us have the mental strength to avoid the 'why me?' question entirely. Soul searching and wallowing in the decision the company has made is a very easy trap to fall into and is a particularly destructive one. The longer you remain in this state of semi-depression the harder it is to dig yourself out and start again. But start again you must.

Being made redundant often feels like a personal slight, but large scale redundancies, like the ones we have seen during the recession, are quite the opposite.

Picking yourself up and moving on is a very difficult process, but also an essential one – and the sooner you start the better. This handbook will guide you through this process, allowing you to identify the positives in your situation and utilise them in order to move on to the next step in your career, wherever and whatever that might be. Achieving these goals will of course require mental toughness and great determination, but this will make your return to work all the more satisfying.

Picking yourself up and getting back on the work wagon requires great mental strength, but the quicker you can do it the easier it is.

An issue that needs addressing early on is the abolition of a myth – redundancy is not a sign of weakness or inadequacy. It is not something to be embarrassed about or to hide from potential employers or your

Redundancy is no longer seen as a sign of inadequacy.

loved ones; this type of stigma in fact disappeared years ago. The fact of the matter is that redundancy is an occupational hazard that is increasingly prevalent in all sectors of employment, and anyone who goes through their entire career without once being exposed to the threat of redundancy is likely to be among the minority.

Almost all of us will experience the threat of redundancy at some point in our careers.

At the time of writing, some four years after the global financial bubble burst, some 1,500 UK employees are still being made redundant every day[1]. The total number of jobs lost during this period is in the high hundreds of thousands. The notion that redundancy is reserved solely for those no longer valued has clearly been eradicated. In fact, analysis of calls to an IT redundancy hotline found that 69% of employees considered the stigma of redundancy to be reduced compared to the 1990s[2]. This is hardly surprising, considering that 84% of callers to the hotline worked in companies where redundancy had already featured.

Even four years after the global financial meltdown, 1,500 UK employees are being let go every day. It is very unlikely therefore that you will be the only one in the redundancy boat at the time.

This shift in attitude has inevitably filtered through to prospective employers – many of whom will have had to let hard-working members of staff go themselves. No longer do recruiters mark a cross against a CV mentioning the word 'redundancy', and being up front and honest about the fact will work much more in your favour than trying to explain it away.

Calls to an IT redundancy hotline found that 69% of employees considered the stigma of redundancy to be reduced compared to the 1990s.

The acknowledgement of the truths of redundancy doesn't of course make the outcome any easier to deal with. Knowing that there are thousands like you and that you won't be pigeonholed when it comes to future job applications doesn't help you feel any better, but it does bring home the point that redundancy is fast becoming a career expectation rather than an exception. If you consider the risk of redundancy as a roulette wheel and each change of company as a ball thrown in, the job hopping nature of the British (see next chapter for further details) means that we are increasing our risk of redundancy far more often. Economic downturns like the ones experienced in the mid-1990s and the late-2000s are no respecter of companies and industries. Like natural disasters they are unpredictable, catastrophic and almost inevitable.

With redundancy now becoming more likely than ever before, it makes sense to be more prepared for it than in previous periods. This book will hopefully enable you to do that – to have a plan of action in place whatever your relationship with redundancy, be it current, potential or a contingency. The fear of redundancy is often worse than the experience itself, and the more prepared you are for it, the less frightening an event it will seem. Whilst it is true that the current job market is oversubscribed, a talented, hard-working individual who displays a desire and drive to get themselves

Prospective employers will have no doubt faced the redundancy question themselves in recent years if not before, so they may be able to empathise with your predicament.

Our job hopping nature means that we are risking the threat of redundancy every two-five years on average. Financial crashes can occur seemingly out of the blue and are no respecter of companies and industries.

It makes sense to have a contingency plan in place in case you are made redundant.

immediately back to work will stand a better chance than someone who lets their joblessness affect their motivation. This is easier said than done, but that is where the preparation comes in – if you have already identified a plan of action you can flick that switch the moment you need to and be a step ahead of the rest. I was made redundant myself some years ago, an experience which has lived with me and provides the backbone for many of the suggestions in this book.

This handbook doesn't just cover the needs of those who want to go straight back into the job market – it also looks at potential opportunities outside your chosen sphere. It may sound like a cliché, but the closing of your individual door can open up others you either never dreamed possible or you wanted to open for years but never had the chance. In other words, being made redundant can represent a new beginning rather than an end. This makes sense if you think about it – suddenly there is nothing stopping you from starting that business, going on that course or even moving abroad to work. Going solo does however carry risks with it, but this is certainly an option worth considering. As you will see from the real life case studies at the end of each section, many people have used their redundancy not as a millstone but as a springboard to the kind of success they would never have enjoyed in their previous jobs. This will not apply

Demystifying redundancy and working out how you might deal with it will make it seem far less forbidding.

Having a plan of action in place will keep you ahead of the rest.

This handbook also looks at opportunities outside your previous sphere of experience. There may be a budding artist in you, just dying to get out!

Many people have found themselves happier, wealthier and more successful following redundancy than they would have done had they stayed in their previous position.

to everyone of course, but those who have always felt a burning desire to do something different may now have that chance.

What this handbook does not cover is the legal framework around which redundancy is based, including your rights and legal challenges through unions etc. This book assumes that you have your leaving card on the mantelpiece, your redundancy pay in your pocket and no plans for Monday morning. The week is your oyster, so let's get started.

Difficult as it may seem to view your redundancy as an opportunity, that is exactly what it represents. The quicker you can get yourself into this mindset the easier and more successful your attempts to get back into work.

This handbook does not cover legal challenges to your redundancy; rather it assumes you are looking toward the future, not trying to change the past.

Clive Lewis

"We are all faced with a series of great opportunities brilliantly disguised as impossible situations."

Charles R Swindoll

"The readiness is all."

William Shakespeare

"Luck is what happens when preparation meets opportunity."

Seneca

Step 1 – The changing world of work

The world of work in the UK was changing well before the financial crashes of the mid-1990s and the late-2000s ushered in new eras of mass redundancy. The gradual decline of production and manufacturing industries coupled with the rise in technology firms and media services has affected the biggest change in the world of work since the industrial revolution. This has had a well publicised effect on employees in associated fields, such as closures of car plants with the related impact on local workers. Gone are the days where a single company or institution provided food for the tables of the majority of the local population. Loyalty and employment stability outweighed personal gain – something almost unimaginable now.

The world of work has changed almost beyond recognition over recent decades.

Manufacturing has gradually made way for technology and internet based industries.

Mutual loyalty between employers and employees seems to belong to the past, and few of us would consider sacrificing personal gain for our employer or manager, unless we were particularly happy there. There are rare cases which prove to be the exception however – in 2007 lottery millionaire Annie Owens shocked her colleagues by staying in her food manufacturing job after her win because she liked her colleagues and employer so much. Similarly, in 2010 ASDA checkout worker Sue Stebbings remained in her job after a £5m lottery win for the same reasons.

Loyalty between employees and employers is becoming increasingly rare, although some extreme cases of loyalty do make the press.

This kind of loyalty however is obviously rare, especially in the younger generation. In 2003 The Office for National Statistics published a report[3] comparing employment figures from 1996 and 2001, illustrating perfectly the way in which the attitude to work in the UK has changed and continues to change. Of interest here, they found that in 1996 half of all employees had been working for the same firm for five years or less. By 2001 it had dropped to four years. The trend for the younger generation to be more active job hoppers was also supported by the figures – 51% of workers in the 18-24 age group were in the same job as 12 months previously compared with 86% of those aged 50 and over. Nine years down the line, in 2010, Gregg and Wadsworth found that 32% of 35-44 year old men were in jobs that had lasted for at least ten years compared to 49% of 55-64 year olds[4]. The concept of a job for life therefore is practically non-existent to contemporary generations of workers, for whom even a career for life is beginning to look doubtful.

Whether employees or employers are to blame for this change is open to debate, but, whatever the root cause, employees now generally consider remaining in the same position with the same skill set for too long as a hindrance to themselves rather than an opportunity to progress within the company.

In 1996, half of all employees had been working for the same firm for five years or less. By 2001 it had dropped to four years.

In 2003, 51% of workers in the 18-24 age group were in the same job as 12 months previously compared with 86% of those aged 50 and over.

In 2010, 32% of 35-44 year old men were in jobs that had lasted for at least ten years compared to 49% of 55-64 year olds.

Effectively by changing jobs so frequently they are casting their net of transferable skills as wide as possible in order to make themselves as recession proof as possible. This does little for continuity and career focus but is more a natural reaction to the times.

Employees generally consider remaining in one job for too long as a hindrance to their progression rather than loyalty to their employer.

Recessions and their repercussions of course magnify the redundancy situation, but in Britain we have to couple this with a government trying to control spiralling debt by cutting back in many public areas. This then increases the risk of redundancy for industries previously thought recession proof, such as teaching and nursing or other roles in the public sector.

An ongoing recession combined with a government trying to tackle huge debt has increased the risk of redundancy in all sectors.

The reason for detailing this rather bleak scenario is to try and reassure you that you're not the odd one out. That redundancy and changing jobs are now a part of working life and, if you are of the older generation of workers, then there is nothing to be feared by redundancy and a potential change in direction. People are living and, crucially, working longer, so unless you are happy and financially secure enough to accept your redundancy package as just that, you still have the time to do something different. Recessions and redundancies will come again, hopefully avoiding you next time, but either way you will be stronger for having gone through this experience and more able to cope should you suffer it again.

Redundancy is now almost an occupational hazard rather than a seismic blow to your career hopes.

Redundancies and recessions come and go. You may just have been one of the unlucky ones.

"Job security is gone. The driving force of a career must come from the individual."

Homa Bahrami

"It is not the strongest of the species that survive, nor the most intelligent, but the one most responsive to change."

Charles Darwin

"It is extremely unlikely that anyone coming out of school with a technical degree will go into one area and stay there. Today's students have to look forward to the excitement of probably having three or four careers."

Gordon Moore

Amy's story

I was working for a large retailer and had just gained a major promotion – a transition from a line manager role into a HR and training role. The company agreed to train me up with a view to further promotions in the HR field, and sure enough after my training I was indeed promoted to the role of Regional HR Officer and Training Officer. It really was my dream job.

Within five months of taking on the role it was announced that the company was being bought out and that all 'head office' staff (as I was categorised) wouldn't be needed any more – a decision made without any consultation. Overnight my world collapsed. I went through a period of disbelief at first – I think I was in denial as to what was happening. I then felt quite a bit of anger, blaming the company on two fronts – firstly for moving me into this new role when I would have been safe in my previous one, and secondly because they must have known about the new owner's plans when I was appointed. I had just bought my first flat and was worried about paying my mortgage and bills. It all felt incredibly unfair. All my recent luck had suddenly reversed itself.

The redundancy seemed to spark the beginning of a sequence of bad luck; shortly afterwards I split up with my boyfriend before my mother was diagnosed with cancer. I was offered a HR role with a subsidiary company, a job which meant a move away from friends and family, but I felt under pressure to get back into work as soon as possible and accepted. It never felt right however, especially with my mother being ill, and after 18 difficult months I left and moved back home. This period brought home the errors in my hasty decision making and lack of planning and made me realise what I truly did and didn't want. Before long I'd been offered a HR position with a highly regarded professional services firm back in London. I was scared of making a second career error, but my soul searching and resultant planning had led me to follow my heart, and this time I made no errors. The role was extremely challenging but it was the start of a new era for me – a ten year one in fact, compared to the six months I originally thought I would spend with the company. I was also repeatedly promoted, allowing me to experience different specialist HR roles.

I still look back at the redundancy and feel that it sent me off-track for those 18 months. However, through following my heart and having the courage to change I was finally able to find something that compares to my original job. I also met my future husband at the new company. Redundancy was not the best time in my life, but I feel that I made the best of it and have emerged as a stronger person.

Step 2 – Handling the news

However the news of your redundancy was presented to you, whether it followed a transparent process or came after weeks of office or even press speculation, dealing with the decision and its ramifications can prove to be a very difficult hurdle to overcome. It is imperative however that you do just this, and as soon as possible.

Moving on isn't easy, but it is essential, and the quicker the better.

The range of reactions and emotions individuals experience upon hearing the news will naturally be different for each; some react with shock and anger whilst others may bypass this and head straight for sadness and a sense of personal failure or embarrassment. This can depend firstly on how the redundancy was handled. In a previous book I talked about the worrying rise in numbers of managers who are afraid of having difficult conversations. Because of this there are therefore a great many people, yourself included perhaps, who were reassured by managers that there would be no redundancies in your department, only to find that you are being called back into the office weeks later to discover the exact opposite. This approach, if I can even call it one, adds a layer of betrayal to the anger and resentment felt by affected individuals, and is the worst possible way to begin such a delicate and taxing process of getting over

Individual reactions to the news will vary, but these are usually variations of shock, anger or worry.

Some managers cover up potential redundancies, which only makes the inevitable worse for everyone.

redundancy and getting back into work. Being told openly and honestly about redundancy doesn't make the shock of it any easier, but it does mean that this sense of betrayal is usually avoided, meaning you only have one set of issues to deal with.

Psychiatrist Elisabeth Kübler-Ross put forward a Grief Cycle in 1969 which outlined the path that many people take when confronted by bad news. A cycle which was originally used for terminally ill patients but has now been adapted as a rule of thumb for any bad news that affects change. You may recognise some of the following stages[5].

Elisabeth Kübler-Ross put forward a Grief Cycle which assesses the steps associated with receiving life changing news.

1. Denial or shock

A feeling of 'this isn't happening' – the brain's attempt to limit potential damage. This feeling is usually only temporary as we quickly realise that our denials are in vain.

Stage 1 – Denial: 'This can't be happening'.

2. Anger

The 'why me?' stage. We often look for someone to blame, be it our boss, colleagues or even fate. Many people at this stage can be difficult to reason with and can seem irrational.

Stage 2 – Anger: 'Why me?'

3. Bargaining

Seeking to alter the decision, offering to do anything for things to remain as they are.

Stage 3 – Bargaining: 'I'll do anything to stay'.

4. Depression

Bargaining has failed and the reality sets in. We realise the losses we are about to incur and what the change will mean for the future. For some, this is a very difficult stage to get out of and is often the most destructive one.

Stage 4 – Depression: 'I'll never get over this'.

5. Acceptance

We realise that fighting the issue is pointless and that there is no choice but to move on. This can turn out to be the first positive step forward, but equally it can be an unhappy time – especially if you have been fighting the decision through tribunals and the like. For some, getting to this stage may take days or weeks. For others it may take months or even years.

Stage 5 – Acceptance: 'It's happened, I can deal with it and move on'.

There are two important additions to note about this model. Firstly, Kübler-Ross discovered that we don't simply follow this path through from point one to point five, rather we cycle between the points – including back to previously 'conquered' stages – without warning. It takes time for our minds to adjust to the reality of redundancy and become philosophical rather than remaining bitter or down about it. Psychological wounds are very much like physical ones in that they take time to heal and any rupture before healing is complete, will open the wound up again. Unfortunately with psychological wounds we cannot easily tell when the healing is complete.

We don't follow this path from start to end, rather we cycle between stages. It is normal to experience setbacks while the emotional wounds heal.

Unfortunately psychological wounds take longer to heal and we cannot always be sure when they have.

Secondly, Kübler-Ross made sure to mention that there is a thread that runs throughout all five stages – hope. The amount of hope you carry with you, be it hope that you will find further employment quickly, that you will be able to pick yourself up and carry on or simply that you will cope well, will aid your healing and limit the amount of 'cycling' that goes on between the stages. This is a very important point. It is easy to lose hope, either when you first hear the news or after you have lived with it for a while, but the moment you do, you surrender the opportunity for change. Maintaining hope is far easier said than done of course, but, as I have said before, meeting redundancy head on from the start and using it as a springboard rather than a trapdoor is the best way to tackle it. Nobody will look down on you for being made redundant, and the fact that you have found work in the past is a very good indicator that you will find it again soon.

Kübler-Ross also mentioned that the amount of hope you carry with you will aid your healing.

It is easy to lose hope as you move through or cycle between the stages, but it may turn out to be a blessing in disguise.

Helen's story

What made my redundancy particularly bad for me was that I genuinely loved my job. I had been approached by the company and had joined with a clear route of progression. I was also the highest earning consultant every year. I had built and grown an established and profitable client base, and even when the recession hit we decided to focus on our strengths and were sure we could see it out.

One Monday morning in December we were gathered in a circle and told that the business was no longer sustainable and that our sister company was no longer prepared to support us. We all sat together, held hands and cried. Being a worrier I couldn't help panicking about my husband and our financial situation. What if I couldn't find work? I'd spent the past two years coaching candidates who had excellent skills but were unable to find roles. I felt guilty, desperate, fearful, vulnerable and angry. I had given my all to the company, and now I felt that they had betrayed me.

Once I'd processed the practical financial side, the hardest thing for me was the loss of the personal relationships. My boss was a warm, tactile woman who I'd turned to for advice on personal issues whilst working with her. We were more than just manager and direct report; she had even laced up my wedding dress! I felt especially betrayed that she had assigned herself as the person to carry on the business, whilst the rest of us were hung out to dry. I lost all respect for her professionally and personally in that moment.

I can now say that, after a year and a half, the redundancy process has changed me. I saw being made redundant as an indication that I had failed (I am my own harshest critic, which didn't help). I confess to still feeling very bitter at my former boss and have no interest at all in re-establishing the once very close relationship we shared. It took me a long time to feel secure of my abilities again. I have always set very high standards for myself and I saw the redundancy as a questioning of my talents. Although I have since found a new role which I enjoy very much, my redundancy cut me very deep and it will take time for these wounds to heal.

"The most effective way to cope with change is to help create it."

L.W. Lynett

"There are times in everyone's life when something constructive is born out of adversity... when things seem so bad that you've got to grab your fate by the shoulders and shake it."

Author Unknown

"If we don't change, we don't grow. If we don't grow, we are not really living."

Lord Chesterfield

Step 3 – Picking yourself up

Redundancy, as we have already seen, is now more or less a fact of working life. This doesn't make it any less traumatic of course, but treating it as a temporary blip in your career path rather than a derailment will help you get back into the right frame of mind to start looking for work. In short, you really have no choice but to get back on the horse again – and the quicker the better. Life goes on, and knowing that there's competition out there should spur you on to get moving sooner. The quicker you can get your head around the idea that redundancy is temporary rather than permanent unemployment, the quicker and easier it will be to pick yourself up and carry on.

Only the most rational of us will take redundancy on the chin, accept it and walk away bearing no ill feeling towards individuals or the company. These people are the lucky ones – and in the extreme minority. The rest of us will feel these negative emotions in varying degrees depending upon the manner of our exit. Being told by well meaning friends to 'stop being negative' often has the opposite effect on our sense of frustration, in the same way that a depressive resents being told to 'cheer up'.

Regardless of how it is delivered though, the truth of the matter is that these negative feelings do indeed act

Knowing that others are in your position doesn't necessarily make you feel any better, but it may spur you on to get things moving quicker if you know there's competition.

Try and view redundancy as temporary unemployment rather than a permanent, negative change of circumstances.

It is natural to experience negativity towards the company or various individuals, but don't let it consume you.

Well meaning friends may tell you to 'cheer up' and that 'it could be worse'. Remember that they mean well!

as a harness to your ability to move on. Deep down we know this, but, as discussed previously, the wounds need to heal before we can move on. It is of course cathartic and, in terms of stress release, almost essential to air your grievances regarding your departure, but it is important to know when the time has come to leave the past in the past and focus on the future instead. Try to think of redundancy as a sideways step in your life journey, rather than a major detour. You have found work before and you'll find it again – perhaps even in a more exciting and fulfilling position than you were in previously (this topic will be discussed later in the book).

By all means vent your frustrations to friends, family and colleagues, but know when to put the past in the past and look to the future.

Prospective employers too will be more impressed with someone who has tried to put their redundancy behind them and started to look to the future, rather than appearing bitter about their treatment and putting off the search. Remember too that there is nothing to stop you searching for work whilst serving your redundancy notice period, although you may lose your right to statutory redundancy pay if you do find other work in this time. I'm sure you'll agree however that this is a small price to pay for the security of a new job. It may sound simple to say that the quicker you start looking for work the better, but in the immediate aftermath of redundancy many find attempting to jump straight back into the world of job hunting taxing

By following the points outlined in this guide you may end up with an even more fulfilling role than you had before.

Prospective employers will look more favourably on someone who has looked to the future, carefully considered their next step and acted professionally.

— especially if you haven't had to do so for a while. Use your notice period wisely, perhaps networking with existing or new contacts in order to explore potential opportunities or lay foundations for something in the future. Until you start knocking on doors you'll never know, and it just takes asking the right person at the right time to make your redundancy even more of a minor stepping stone. As well as speaking to existing or potential contacts, speak to those who are also going through what you're going through. This could mean asking someone who has previously experienced redundancy for advice or guidance, staying in contact with former colleagues, promising to look out for fellow redundancy sufferers (two pairs of eyes are better than one) and registering with related websites and forums. Not only will you find suggestions and opportunities that you may never have thought of yourself, liaising with others in the same boat will help to demystify redundancy.

Before moving onto the next step I would like you to perform a task. Using the related page at the back of the book (page 100), list the skills and attributes you could offer an employer — those aspects of your personality and skill base that are your 'added value' as an employee — and the types of activities that you are not good at or not interested in doing. Think inside as well as outside the box — everything counts. Don't be

During your redundancy notice period, try networking with new or existing contacts and colleagues.

Speak to others who are going or have gone through what you are experiencing. Visit websites and forums and ask around.

List your skills, competencies and what you can offer a prospective employer. Don't be modest!

modest either. You will need to sell yourself in the coming weeks, so get used to reeling off your strengths and areas of expertise. Not only is this task important in the effectiveness of this book, but it can also remind you what you have to offer and can give you a timely morale boost. Once you have finished, read the list back to yourself a number of times. Indulge in your abilities. Really get to know what you can offer employers. Don't be shy about it – revel in it!

This list of skills and attributes is a personal sales kit. Learn it and believe in it – you'll need it!

Toby's story

I had been working for a telecoms firm for seven years and had worked my way up from customer service representative to customer service team leader. I loved the company, the people and the relaxed attitude – it was right up my street. We were all aware that the company had been struggling a little, but as far as we knew they were going to sell another less profitable arm of the business and continue on the established areas. It was a complete shock therefore when my fellow team leaders and I were called into the manager's office and told that 25% of the customer service workforce was going to be let go, including us. This was, naturally, a very tense time.

Over the following weeks, a series of interviews were conducted with team members from all levels, the upshot of which was that, with me being one of the more recent additions to the managerial team, I was one of the first to go. I was utterly devastated. I knew that I would never find an office, workforce or company like that again, and it felt as if my luck had simply run out. It was odd to think that had I stayed in my previous post I probably would have kept my job and that my promotion turned out to be my undoing. My manager was extremely helpful and fought for a decent redundancy package for me, but there were plenty of tears when I finally left. I wasn't angry at anybody as such, just upset at what I was leaving and how it had come about.

After a spell of near depression I was pushed by friends and family to make some positive steps forward. I registered my CV on some job websites, but didn't really make much of an effort. It wasn't until I got a call from a similar telecoms company that I started to think more positively; they had seen my CV on a website and were considering me for a role. The salary turned out to be too low but it gave me the confidence to contact other similar companies directly. I did this, aiming my enquiries at the customer service departments, and after sending out about 20 communications I was finally contacted by a competitor of my former company who offered me an identical position to the one I had left. The salary was slightly lower but the package was still attractive. Whilst they weren't quite as laid back as my previous employer, the job offer was nevertheless a no-brainer. I joined them and have gained one promotion since. I'm still nervous about my chances of being made redundant again, but I'm determined not to let it hold me back. I'm still in contact with some of my previous colleagues, which makes for interesting banter!

"You can conquer almost any fear if you will only make up your mind to do so. For remember, fear doesn't exist anywhere except in the mind."

Dale Carnegie

"An invincible determination can accomplish almost anything and in this lies the great distinction between great men and little men."

Thomas Fuller

"Confront your fears, list them, get to know them, and only then will you be able to put them aside and move ahead."

Jerry Gillies

Step 4 – Exploring the options

Hopefully by this stage your redundancy should be starting to seem more like a past event than a current or future concern. You are confident in what you can offer an employer and you believe in your abilities. Now it's time to start finding work.

Your options may seem limited now, but the time you take to re-evaluate your career may prove more important than you think.

The first stepping stones on the route back to work are preceded by a potential pitfall that you must first negotiate. Of course none of us can predict what is round the corner, and we can only work in the short space of time between our redundancy being announced and the bank balance dropping too much, but many job seekers err by rushing headlong into the first remotely suitable job offer they receive, regardless of certain crucial aspects. Whilst on the point of money, it is a good idea to make a note of all your outgoings to see how long you will be able to survive until you need to be back in work. As you do this, you may find regular outgoings such as an old gym membership or out of date subscriptions can be eliminated. Naturally, financial requirements will play a huge part in your decision making. It may help to calculate what the absolute minimum you need to earn is in order to get by and then balance further earnings with your intentions in the work/life balance area. Again, this all depends on what your evaluated life

Don't rush into the first job you're offered, unless you already know a great deal about the company, the role and the industry.

Considering your long-term options really is the best way to make your redundancy work for you.

goals are. For example, less pressure may mean less money but equally more family time. Which is really important to you? Making these evaluations will help you to manage your outgoings more effectively. Don't be afraid to be ruthless. Think of it as a business exercise. Every penny counts!

Redundancy offers you a great chance to take stock of your situation and consider your work/life balance.

Desperation for work may lead you to overlook things like location, role, chances of promotion and even the type of work you will be doing, but this will often, as you can imagine, have further negative effects later on. Of course some jobs you may see instinctively are right for you, but accepting something in a different sphere altogether is a risk sometimes not worth taking. Considering your long-term options may initially seem like wasted time, but you will not get the opportunity to re-evaluate your working life in such a manner again for some time. Here is how to make the most of it (it may help to keep your newly made 'skills list' handy here).

Did you work too much in your previous job?

Would you like to see more of your friends/family, take up a new hobby or pursue existing interests?

Do you want to work closer to home?

Personal options

As I have already mentioned, redundancy is a great opportunity to sit back and take stock of what you want out of life and whether anything needs changing. The work/life balance is something many of us fail to achieve properly, but redundancy is a good opportunity to do just this. If you had a job that

It may help to discuss these questions with loved ones and those most affected.

involved long hours or working weekends, was it suitable or would you prefer more leisure time? Do you see your family and friends as much as you wish? Do you want to work closer to home? Asking questions of this type may bring surprising answers and will immediately help you focus your search. Of course there may be factors in your life that mean change can't be facilitated wholesale (family responsibilities, travel costs etc.), but there are bound to be some areas for improvement. The opinions of others are always useful here if you think you're either stuck or, conversely, think you can now have the free and easy life!

Financial requirements will naturally limit your options, but consider what you can feasibly live on and then factor any extra earnings around your revised work/life balance (extra money means extra time and pressure).

Also think about what type of work you enjoy and what type of employer you want to work for. Do you enjoy being practical, analytical or creative? Do you thrive or wilt under pressure? Do you enjoy or abhor fierce competition? All these questions will help shape and reveal the kind of work you enjoy which, when married up with your identified skills and areas of strength, should produce a number of options.

There are commonly six areas of work to consider.

Employment options

When it comes to the types of work out there, your options are commonly divided into six sections which are discussed next.

The most common type of employment is **permanent** work. You will probably be familiar with permanent jobs, be they full-time or part-time. They are intended as long-term jobs with no predestined end date. They provide the most security, stability and regular income but bring with them a possible lack of variety and flexibility.

Permanent work: Long-term jobs with no predetermined end date. More security and stability, but less variety and flexibility.

Temporary or **contract** work, either full-time or part-time, is work that carries with it a specific end date – although this can be extended or made permanent. People generally move from contract to contract every few months or have more than one going at once. Contract work provides more variety and a flexible working pattern, but brings with it a risk of periods of unemployment, irregular income and fewer benefits.

Temporary/contract work: Work with a predetermined end date (i.e. six months/one year). Provides more flexibility but brings risk of unemployment and irregular income.

Self-employment is not for the faint hearted. Many people like the idea of being their own boss but few realise what it actually entails. Running your own business can be immensely satisfying and can be achieved in almost any field you choose, from consultancy work to running a franchise to being a plumber. It offers independence, job satisfaction, flexibility and potentially high earnings but demands very hard work with the risk of little initial reward, loss of security and benefits (pension, legal rights, paid holiday) and potential isolation for long periods.

Self-employment: Being your own boss, from consultant to builder, brings independence, freedom and a huge sense of achievement but risks include little early reward and loss of security and benefits.

A combination of different roles such as part-time positions, self-employment or voluntary work, is known as a **portfolio career**. They are increasing in popularity and offer variety, flexibility and the chance to broaden your skill base but carry with them irregular income, lack of security and loss of traditional rights and benefits.

Portfolio career: A combination of different positions (self-employment, voluntary and part-time work). Brings flexibility and variety but lacks security and employment rights.

Alternative lifestyles will suit far less people than the previous areas outlined, but for those in a position to accept, they can be the most satisfying. Alternative lifestyles can involve public appointments (sitting on advisory bodies, tribunals or public corporations), or voluntary work. Many find the challenge, the personal reward, the independence and the opportunity to grow enjoyable, but beware the time required to achieve your new goals, the loss of earnings and the odd hours.

Alternative lifestyles: Public appointments, voluntary work or retirement. Brings personal rewards and independence, but frequently brings dramatic decrease in earnings and odd hours.

As well as these six styles of work, consideration should also be given to what kind of industries are more likely to prosper in the near to middle future. You will of course want to make yourself as recession proof as possible now, a big part of which involves working in lower risk sectors. There is naturally no way of predicting which these are in the long-term, but the recent recessions have hit industries in the **primary** and **secondary** sectors hardest (e.g. manufacturing and farming). **Tertiary** and **quaternary** sectors (service

Primary and secondary industries (farming, manufacturing etc.) are in decline and often suffer in recessions.

providers, science/technology research) have also been hit although not as hard, and are generally better equipped to handle financial downturns. They are not immune of course, but the skills associated with work of this type are also more highly sought after and more transferable.

Tertiary and quaternary industries (service providers, science/tech research, internet etc.) represent more stable employment and more transferable skills.

Hand in hand with this type of sector comes another question to consider – **public** or **private**. Naturally some jobs will immediately decide this for you as far as this goes (e.g. investment banker, council administrator), but a change of sector may be something you hadn't considered although may like the idea of. It is worth researching the pros and cons of both before making a decision however, as the appeal may be different from the reality! There is indeed the option of taking some time out totally and volunteering in the third sector, nonetheless I won't be covering this in detail in this book, given that the majority of people will be interested in returning to paid employment.

Consider which sector you'd like to work in – public or private. You may fancy a change, but research them thoroughly before committing.

Matching up your skills (see end of step 3) with all of the options and ideas above should give you a very clear idea of what you want out of life and your next job – something you probably haven't had the chance to do for a while. When you've finally got all this information together, you're ready to enter the job market.

Match these considerations up with your listed skills and attributes to find your ideal career direction.

Jane's story

In 1990, after ten years in Further Education, I moved to a newly created job with a relatively new organisation. I had been there for a year or so when we began to explore a merger with a neighbouring organisation. The general view was that we were the stronger in terms of customer service, effective systems etc., so it was quite a shock when, in the middle of these exploratory talks, our CEO suddenly left to take up a new job, with very little explanation as to why he had decided to leave.

Two weeks or so into his post, our new CEO was faced with telling a group of people he barely knew that the organisation was no longer financially viable and that we were all to be made redundant. I remember sitting around a table in a small room with the other members of staff, the CEO and three board members, only one of whom seemed to display any emotional sympathy for us as individuals. I recall that we were all in tears and didn't know how to react, but nobody from the company offered us any support. The formal process kicked in, and very shortly we were all on our own. I started to feel angry and resentful because I knew I had been doing a good job and I wanted to carry on doing it – it was almost a process of grieving for the opportunities I'd lost.

Subsequent feelings were worry and self-doubt. I was the main wage earner with an 18 year old daughter at college and a ten year old son and I was concerned that, at the age of 50, I might be considered too old for a dynamic and challenging career. I was also out of practice with job applications and interviews, and we had been given no support or advice on this during the redundancy period. When I started looking for jobs it was hard to find anything remotely appealing. The one job I liked the look of was a 12 month contract offering less than half my previous salary. I did find one suitable vacancy, and actually interviewed for it, but any acceptance would have been for purely financial reasons. As it was, I wasn't offered the position. Maybe they could sense that I didn't really want it.

Eventually I tackled my situation in a slightly unusual manner; I took a gamble and got back in touch with the new CEO and asked for a meeting, during which I managed to persuade him that my help would be essential in retaining all the customers from the previous organisation and in improving and growing the business. I asked for a chance to prove my worth and was initially given a one year contract with a clear brief of keeping all existing clients. Not only did I achieve this but I also attracted substantial new business and have remained with the company as a manager ever since. I suppose you could say that I thought outside the box, but really I knew what I wanted and what I was good at and I played to my strengths.

Looking back, I see that the experience of being made redundant felt threatening and isolating – the people I thought had my interests at heart let me down and friends and family, no matter how sympathetic, inevitably appeared to be much better off than me. Although it may be entirely illogical, it is hard to shake off the feeling that you have failed personally and therefore everyone else will see that you are a failure. I think that, at the very least, anyone going through this experience should be offered both practical help with finances, writing job applications and the like and emotional help through counselling or mentoring. After all, it's a lonely place to be.

"When people go to work, they shouldn't have to leave their hearts at home."

Betty Bender

"Opportunity is missed by most people because it is dressed in overalls and looks like work."

Thomas Edison

"Looking back at the times where I allowed my work to create stress and frustration in my life I now realise what I thought was important really was not. I am not saying you should not take your work seriously, what I am saying is that we need to realise that life is all about balance."

Catherine Pulsifer

Step 5 – The visible job market

The visible job market is the one we all know – external advertisements (newspapers, internet etc.), recruiters (headhunters and agencies) and online jobsites. The advantage to these visible methods is that the role, requirements and salary are all known up front, but the disadvantage is that thousands or even millions of people may be pursuing the same avenue.

The visible job market consists of advertised jobs, recruiters and online jobsites.

The process for applying for **advertised jobs** varies but should be clearly stated on each advert. As with any type of submission, ensure that your CV and covering letter are tailored for each individual job you apply for. This may seem like a laborious process, but with so many people applying for jobs you need to tick as many boxes as possible – something that can only be achieved if you directly match up your skills and experiences with the unique requirements of each job. A little effort here can bring a lot of reward whilst laziness or lack of attention to detail can be costly.

We are all familiar with advertised jobs in their various forms – be they in newspapers and journals or online. Ensure that your CV and covering letter are tailored for each job application.

Before leaping into a decision to apply for a job, ensure you have clearly read and understood the specifications of the role – including reading between the lines. Some recruiters may try to camouflage less desirable elements of the job, so be careful. If possible, speak to the recruiter before applying. This could be a genuine call to confirm details about the job spec, but

Ensure you read and understand the job spec before applying. Some unscrupulous advertisers may try to camouflage undesirable elements of the job.

don't let a lack of questions hold you back; find a reason to call them and do so. The aim here is to plant a seed in the recruiter's head of how keen, professional and genuine you sound on the phone so that when your CV comes through they remember you. An initial polite, pleasant and professional phone call may just bump you up the list a little. At any rate, it's worth a try.

Find an excuse to call the recruiter so they can get a better feel for who you are. Hopefully they'll remember you when your CV comes through.

A second side to the visible market is the world of **agencies**. Agencies in various markets have boomed in recent years, with the result that competition in many parts of the country is cut-throat. This competition is of major benefit to you as a candidate, given that consultants often have great recruitment networks and earn their living by getting people like you jobs. There are three types of recruiter, all of which work slightly differently.

There are now agencies for almost every area of work, from junior to senior positions. This competitive market is great for candidates.

High street agencies tend to work with more junior roles and match up candidates they think can be placed with existing vacancies that have to be filled. You walk into the branch or register on their website, the recruiter determines whether they think they can place you before registering you and you go from there. It is common practice to call an agency once a week or so if you haven't heard from them, just to remind them that you're still looking, but don't

High street agencies usually work with more junior roles.

Registering with more than one agency is advisable, but always be honest with them about your job hunt developments.

bombard them. Remember – they make money from getting you a job, so they will be looking.

Headhunters use company briefs to search the market for suitable candidates. They use their contacts and researchers to identify targets which they then present to the client to choose from. Approaching a headhunter yourself will occasionally yield results, but, due to the nature of their work, they will often turn down applicants. If you are of a senior level, making headhunters in your chosen sphere aware of your skills and availability might not be a bad idea – assuming that you want to stay in that field. The reality is, if you are making an impact (or have made one) in your organisation and particularly your industry, it is likely that some may already be aware of you.

Selection consultants receive a brief from a company, create a person specification and job advertisement and then publish them on appropriate websites or in appropriate publications. They then collate the best applicants, shortlist them and present them to the company for final selection. As the description suggests, you may only ever come into contact with them through adverts.

Finally, **jobsites** are online mediums where jobseekers upload their CVs for recruiters to search and respond to recruiter adverts. There are specialist jobsites and

Headhunters recruit for more senior roles and will usually find you rather than you approaching them. If you are of a senior level however, it can't hurt to make headhunters in relevant industries aware of your position.

Selection consultants work on company briefs to come up with a person specification and a job advert, which they then place, filter candidates and present a shortlist to the client.

Jobsites are an online medium where recruiters and candidates can register, interact and post/apply for jobs.

general jobsites, so make sure you choose carefully and, again, tailor your CV accordingly. Treat your online profile professionally (i.e. no silly photos) and don't be afraid to contact registered businesses you like the look of. After all, they're on the site for a reason.

Treat your online profile with as much professionalism as your other communications with potential employers. And don't be scared to contact those you like the look of either.

Clive Lewis

Claudia's story

I had been with a telecoms organisation for 18 months as head of HR. With the overseas based parent company looking at flotation, a new HR Director was brought in to manage the process and ensure the organisation could sustain the scrutiny and rigours of due diligence. A few months later I was asked to attend a meeting with my immediate boss at our Bristol office. At this meeting we were informed that the layers of HR staff were to be reduced and as such my post was now redundant. I had already wondered how the new HR structure would work, but I was shocked that this meeting was the first (and only) discussion on the subject and wasn't in fact a discussion but a 'fait accompli'. I felt let down, angry and unappreciated. It simply wasn't fair. I was offered paid notice and a lump sum and didn't feel I had any recourse to challenge the decision. My experience of managing the redundancy of other people counted for little, and I felt totally deflated. It was all very personal and entirely out of my control. With the benefit of hindsight, I realise I was rather politically naïve when the new boss had talked to me as part of his induction; I think I had been too honest about my views on HR and he may have seen me as disruptive.

The embarrassment of having to go in and collect my possessions was terrible, as was telling people I had been made redundant. The suddenness of the process really knocked my self-confidence, but as time went on I sought out colleagues and professional support and this helped me move on.

I ended up being out of work for about six months. During this time I reassessed what I wanted out of a job and what new skills I needed to acquire to achieve my new aims. I took a number of short summer courses at my local college and met lots of new people, deciding eventually to do an MBA to broaden my HR skills. Shortly afterwards I was contacted by a headhunter about a HR Directorship role. I interviewed and was not only offered the post but also offered funding for my MBA on a part-time basis. I now run my own business which specialises in executive coaching and coaching supervision, leadership team development and board effectiveness. I think my own experience of being made redundant really helped me understand the pressures that today's executives' face and the benefits of taking hold of your own career planning. Although it was a painful process, it offered me the chance to proactively manage my career, which I otherwise would not have been able to do. In the long-term it certainly worked out for the better.

"Keep asking until you find the answers. In sales there are usually four or five 'no's' before you get a 'yes'."

Jack Canfield

"When defeat comes, accept it as a signal that your plans are not sound, rebuild those plans, and set sail once more toward your coveted goal."

Napoleon Hill

"Perseverance is the hard work you do after you get tired of doing the hard work you already did."

Newt Gingrich

Step 6 – The hidden job market

Estimates suggest that some 80% of jobs are not advertised, which is incredible when you consider that national recruitment agencies often feature hundreds of thousands of jobs at one time. So how do you get access to these 'hidden' jobs? Sadly there is no easy answer, but the secret lies with being proactive in your approach, using your network of friends, clients and colleagues and contacting companies directly.

Some 80% of jobs are not advertised. The rest are filled through existing contacts, direct approaches and internal promotions.

Networking is the most common method of obtaining jobs in the hidden market. Networking success can sometimes come down to the personality of the individual – some find it natural and some find it difficult – but once you know the do's and don'ts and meet with the odd success or two you will think nothing of it.

Networking is the best way to crack the hidden market. You don't have to have high-powered contacts, but you should be aware of who best to approach and how to do so.

Once you have assessed your options and chosen your career direction using the steps outlined previously, head to your address book or handheld device and identify around ten desirable contacts. At the same time, ensure that former colleagues, clients and friends know that you're available for work and what you are looking for. Social networking sites such as Facebook, Twitter and LinkedIn can also be utilised for these means. Be careful not to sound desperate though –

Ensure that former colleagues and associates, friends and clients know that you are being made redundant. Use social networking tools such as Facebook, Twitter and LinkedIn to advertise the fact.

potential employers can often find this information too.

Once you have identified your first round of contacts, it's time to approach them. Your method of contact will depend on the type of relationship you have – phone calls are suitable for closer relationships but you will probably find yourself emailing more than phoning. There are a couple of rules you should abide by in order to make your canvassing as successful as possible. Firstly, don't ask for a job directly. This may make the conversation somewhat awkward as your contact may feel like you are just using them to look for work. Mentioning your redundancy is fine, in fact it is a good idea to get it out of the way early on, but make it clear that you are only seeking advice and information as to your next steps and who it may be worth contacting, not job hunting directly.

The chances of getting a job directly off the back of these initial calls are limited, but you may be given referrals to those who may be able to help. Follow these referrals up within a few days with a written introduction, again making clear that you are only after information and advice. Outlining your strengths, qualities and experience and asking what this new contact might suggest is a very good way of discreetly advertising yourself to them. Don't be tempted to send in your CV unless requested – this will put you firmly in

Identify around ten 'first choice' contacts and approach them regarding their thoughts on what you should do or where you should go. Avoid asking them directly if they know of positions available.

Consider carefully whether emailing or phoning is the best means of initial contact.

The most likely outcome is that you will be given another name to contact. Follow this up within a few days.

Again, don't be obvious but mention your strengths and experience and ask their advice. This is a discreet form of self-promotion.

the 'job hunting' camp. There is no harm in following up emails after a week if you have received no reply, but don't hassle them. They are doing you a favour after all. If you strike it lucky and a contact comes good then the standard recruitment wheels will get into motion from there, meaning it's time to work on your CV and interviewing skills (see later steps).

Follow up unanswered emails or unreturned calls after a few days, but remember that they are doing you a favour so don't hassle them.

The other approach to breaking into the hidden market is **direct contact**. This is the 'cold-calling' side of the recruitment world, and as such takes more time, effort and luck than using existing networks. However, the right approach at the right time may pay dividends.

Direct contact means sending your CV and covering letter to companies direct. It requires more time and effort and positive results are fewer than using contacts, but you only need to be lucky once.

To begin with, put together a list of companies you would like to work for and who you suspect may at some point have opportunities that would suit your experience, direction and skill set. Research these companies as much as possible to find any recent contracts they may have won, new offices they may have opened or have planned, even any departures that may have made the news. Essentially, try and find any potential gap in the company that you feel you could fill. If you find something appropriate, mention this specifically in your approach letter. If not, don't worry.

Research complete, find the name of the person who deals with recruitment in the area you want to target and send them your CV and covering letter (see step 8 for more details on this). If you don't hear anything back within a week, follow-up with a phone call to see if the letter was received and if there is anything suitable on the horizon. If you are told there are no vacancies, ask how you should find out about vacancies in the future and if you can be kept on file. Keep a note of the name of this person – people change jobs, and a phone call a matter of weeks down the line may yield a different name who won't be aware of you, thus allowing you to try again.

There is no winning formula to approaching companies directly. The secret is thorough research, a professional approach and a bit of fortunate timing. If they have something for you, great. If not, move on to the next company. Don't get downbeat at rejections and lack of contact – just keep plugging away. Luck is often no more than the product of hard work and persistence.

Remember that people change jobs, so the person you contact may not be in that position in a few weeks' time. This means you can try again

Luck can play a part in the success of direct contacting, but persistence and hard work will increase your chances of a lucky break

Ann's story

Until a few years prior, redundancy was practically unheard of in my firm. I worked for one of the largest employers in the county, with offices in the UK, Ireland, Canada, Australia and New Zealand. There was a firm belief and perception that ours were jobs for life. I had worked for the company in various roles for 26 years, working finally in the training department. We had just undergone another of many reviews, but this time we were all sure that bad news was coming our way. We were right – the company had decided to outsource the department. I was devastated. I had spent what felt like a lifetime working hard for the same company. I was reliable and well thought of. Being unemployed was something I could not even contemplate. I had always been in work, even holding down my full-time job plus two part-time jobs to save for a new car.

Following the announcement I did not venture into any of the other offices or even into town on my lunch break, I was so embarrassed about being made redundant. I felt it was about me and not my position. In actual fact to this day I still avoid the centre of town around lunch hours for fear of meeting someone. The mention of the company still makes my stomach churn, and I cannot help but feel slightly bitter towards some of the staff that still work there. On the plus side, my line manager, who was also being made redundant, was absolutely marvellous. He had been in the position a number of times himself before and understood how I felt. Other senior members of the company were less than helpful however, a fact acknowledged when I received an email from the company admitting to 'getting it wrong for me' and learning from their mistakes.

The recession had just started so jobs were not as easy to come by, which was compounded by the fact that I had not had an interview for almost 30 years. Things had changed so much that the thought of an interview was terrifying. I used my network and was approached by an old contact who offered me a job with an immediate start. Whilst it was a complete change of career I felt I had nothing to lose – and very few other options. I stayed there for around three years and only recently left for a new role. I still cannot shake off the effects of being made redundant however, and I am not sure if I ever will.

"It's all about people. It's about networking and being nice to people and not burning any bridges… in the end it is people that are going to hire you."

Mike Davidson

"It isn't just what you know, and it isn't just who you know. It's actually who you know, who knows you, and what you do for a living."

Bob Burg

"If you are not moving closer to what you want in sales (or in life), you probably aren't doing enough asking."

Jack Canfield

Step 7 – Best practice

Dealing with two job markets, dozens of application forms, numerous CVs and various recruiters will inevitably lead to mistakes. Some mistakes are small and largely inconsequential, but many of the bigger ones are easily avoided.

The first mistake many people make is often a panic response to redundancy – blanket applications. You may think that registering with multiple agencies, applying for any and all jobs in your salary bracket and firing off CVs to all the companies in your postal code may increase your chances of success. In fact the reverse is often true. Of course your chances of getting an interview are higher, but the risks of confusion, multiple interviews and agency suspicion mean that clashing or even missed appointments are increasingly likely. There is also the risk of having too many interviews to handle at one time, meaning that you may spread yourself too thin, scrimp on research and interview badly. This lack of research can manifest itself even if you are successful at an interview and get a job – you may fail to ask key questions or understand the role properly. Result? You quickly become unhappy and want to leave. Blanket applications also usually means the cardinal sin of sending untailored CVs and covering letters is committed on a frequent basis.

When dealing with so many people, communications and businesses you will undoubtedly make mistakes. You can, however, make life much easier for yourself in a number of ways.

Don't be tempted to blanket apply for jobs. This will likely lead to untailored CVs and covering letters going to a multitude of companies with no strategy in place.

Canvassing too many companies at once can lead to confusion, mistakes and a lack of adequate research.

Instead of this saturation approach, use your personal and professional ambitions and your chosen industrial sectors to search for jobs you know you want and will do well in. You can always alter your expectations and required salary and widen your field of search if you meet with no success, but starting off in this manner will often produce much more satisfactory results.

As we have seen, employment agencies can be useful given their contacts and experience, but many people register with upwards of four at a time – sometimes lying if they are asked that exact question by the next in line. Employment agencies can be jealous beasts and don't like it if you register with competitors without telling them. It is courtesy to inform them of any relevant change in your circumstances – a courtesy which will be rewarded when they speak to companies on your behalf. Give them something good to say. Try and stick to a maximum of four agencies at one time, but equally don't feel under pressure to accept the first job they offer you. They want to make a sale after all, and some less scrupulous ones may try and squeeze you in anywhere to get their commission. Stick to your guns and they'll soon get the message.

Many people also become unstuck through poor planning; they fire off letters to various companies without tracking what they have sent to whom and when, so when it comes to chasing up time, their

Use your revised career goals to identify companies and industries you want to work for. You can always alter your expectations later.

Avoid registering with more than four agencies at once to avoid confusion and potential overburden.

Inform agencies if you have registered with a competitor and remain courteous even if they haven't found you any jobs. Give them good things to say about you.

Don't feel under pressure to accept the first job an agency offers you. They want to make a sale after all. Stick to your career goals until you feel the time may be right to accept a different role.

records are a mess and they end up calling some people twice and forgetting others. Simply keeping a track of what was sent to whom, when and what progress has been made will allow you to easily track any follow-up calls you need to make and will eliminate the risk of over calling and forgetting.

Planning from the outset is key. Keep a record of what you have sent to whom and when. This makes follow-up calls much easier to plan and execute.

A mistake many people make that severely hampers their efforts is sticking to one job market or one approach only – e.g. they only apply for online jobs and ignore networking, direct contact and recruitment agencies. To gain maximum results you must aim to utilise all avenues as equally as possible. Of course some may not have the confidence or capacity to network while others may see applying for external jobs as a waste of time, but spreading your bets across all platforms gives you maximum exposure to the market and therefore the highest chance of success. Again, planning is crucial here, but doing it from the outset will make life much easier than starting when you begin to get somewhere.

Try to spread your campaign over as many avenues as possible – network, approach directly, register with agencies and apply for advertised jobs. Spreading your bets will heighten your exposure to the market.

Finally, consider your online footprint. You would be surprised at just how much information search engines can dig up about you – information employers can locate just as easily. Studies suggest that up to 80% of employers research prospective candidates online, so pre-empt them by doing a little digging yourself. If you uncover anything you don't like the look of either

Consider your online footprint. Uncovering information about you is easier for a prospective employer than you think.

change it yourself if you have the capacity or contact the website owner and ask them to remove the content if possible. Out of date or dead pages can remain in search engine caches and can therefore still be accessed for a time afterwards, but the major ones also operate cached page removal services, if you are concerned about this. Of course you can't cover up everything, and employers don't expect you to be an angel, but cleaning up your online act prior to your campaign could avoid some potentially difficult questions later on.

Try searching for your own name and see what comes up. If you see something you don't want potential employers to see, contact the webmaster to see if you can have it removed – unless you can remove it yourself.

Clive Lewis

Maureen's story

I had been working as a bookkeeper for a small roofing supplies company for some 15 years when I was made redundant. With no real qualifications I had worked extremely hard to earn my place in the company, often requiring 60-70 hour weeks, even though I had two young children, one of whom has special needs. After more than a decade of sacrifice and hard work a colleague and I were promoted to Finance Director level, alongside three male colleagues. Then out of the blue we were informed the roofing and building side of the business was to be sold. This was devastating news. We were obviously concerned about our future and a period of uncertainty began, during which time the acquisition team descended on the premises and began their takeover.

At this point I had about ten accounts staff reporting to me, but they were immediately told that they were no longer to do so. These former subordinates quickly began to ignore me and eventually took full control of the day to day running of the business. I was told that my employment would be terminated within three months, that I would receive statutory redundancy payment and that I was expected to work the notice period. Needless to say I was distraught. I was upset about the timing, shocked at the speed at which events were taking place and angered at the dismissive attitude of the new owners. Working during my notice period was difficult. I hated going into the office each day faced with no work and little contact with anyone. The days were long, boring and an utter waste of my time. On one occasion I noticed that new staff were incorrectly inputting data into the computer system. I tried to point this out but they would not accept what I was saying and politely told me to keep my nose out of things, before sheepishly returning for advice after I was proved correct. I was tempted to make a claim for unfair dismissal, but didn't want to take action during the period in which I was still working – I was already being badly treated, and this would only make things worse. It transpired however that there was a three month time limit for making a claim so I was too late to do so.

After leaving I had four job offers. I decided to take a slight departure and took a post as a veterinary practice manager. This turned out to be a bad decision and I left after 18 months. I took a six month break to revaluate things before commencing my current job as an administration/HR manager, a job I love and hope to do until I decide to retire. I'm almost 58 years old but can't see myself retiring through choice for at least another ten years. The business has gone through many changes and, although there have been further redundancy scares, I am a lot wiser from past experiences. I remain loyal and committed and work longer hours when necessary but redundancy taught me that whatever you have done in the past is soon forgotten when hard decisions need to be made. I now make sure I have more of a work/life balance so that I can enjoy my family life more than I did, which is something that redundancy helped me realise.

"Organising is what you do before you do something, so that when you do it, it is not all mixed up."

A.A. Milne

"Don't spread yourself too thin. Learn to say no politely and quickly."

St. Francis de Sales

"Around 43% of employers said what they had seen on social networking sites had caused them not to hire the candidate."

CareerBuilder.co.uk survey, Jan 2010

Step 8 – Your CV & covering letter

Your CV and covering letter package is your personal sales pitch and its aim is to get you to the first stage of the recruitment process, be that an interview, a meeting or a simple phone conversation with the company or agency in question. For many however, writing or updating a CV and covering letter is an unpleasant or even daunting task. Knowing what to include, what to leave out and how to phrase everything succinctly, yet with an impact, leaves many wondering just where to start. This may especially be the case for someone who hasn't needed to update their CV for some time.

Put together a list of companies, research them and contact the relevant department with your CV and covering letter. Mention any gaps in the company you may have found during your research that you think you can fill.

This section looks at the CV and the covering letter individually and should help you get a basic idea of how to go about creating a winning application package.

Covering letter

A covering letter is read before a CV and should act as an incentive for the reader to want to read your CV. If the covering letter makes no impression they may not even get that far. Like the CV, this document should be tailored to the job and should reflect but not mirror what is stated in your CV. Mention one or two of your highest and most relevant achievements to impress the reader – don't hide them away in your CV.

The covering letter should start with the obvious – why you are writing to the company. If you don't mention what you want from them how are they going to know? If you are applying for a vacancy, mention how you came to know about it.

Start your covering letter by saying why you are writing and, if you are responding to a vacancy, how you came across it.

Next, mention in a couple of sentences why you are the best person for the job. Don't boast, but don't undersell yourself. Mention your experience, training and maybe a star success or two to hook the reader into continuing.

Without boasting, say why you are suitable for the position. Mention relevant experience, training and successes.

Refer them next to your enclosed CV and state very clearly when you are available for interview (usually this will be at their 'earliest convenience'). Finally, thank them for their time and consideration and say that you look forward to hearing from them. If posting, ensure also that both the covering letter and CV are in as pristine condition as they can possibly be. All these small factors reflect on your professionalism.

Refer the reader to your enclosed CV and state when you are available for interview.

If posting, ensure that your covering letter and CV are stain free!

CV

Whilst there is no single right CV there are plenty of wrong ones out there; rather, there are plenty of mistakes that people make. First and foremost, as I have already discussed, your CV should always be tailored to the type of job and company you had in mind. If you only have one CV which you send to every company regardless of their requirements then you are highly unlikely to hear back from many of them, if any.

There are typically three types of CV for you to consider. The **performance** CV is the most common and the one you will likely be using yourself. It lists your employment history first, starting with your most recent position, and lists your roles, responsibilities and achievements within those roles. These achievements should be relevant to the company and job you are applying for. Performance CVs are often used by those wishing to remain in the same sector.

A **skills based** CV should be used if you have had a varied or broken up career or if you want to change direction. The focus should be on your transferable skills and competencies rather than the companies you worked for and the positions you held. This enables recruiters to see at a glance how your experience and skills match the needs of the job or the company. Consider areas such as team and leadership skills, communication skills, problem solving skills and creative skills.

Alternative or **portfolio based** CVs are mainly used by senior managers or those looking for freelance or creative positions. As the name suggests they are

There are some common mistakes that people make on their CVs, the most common being neglecting to tailor it to the company and the job in question.

*A **performance** CV is most common to those applying for work in their current or most recent sector. It focuses on your positions, roles and responsibilities and runs in chronological order.*

*A **skills based** CV is for those who, for whatever reason, have a varied or broken up career. The focus should be on transferable skills which recruiters can match to their requirements.*

usually backed up by a portfolio of work which, to a certain extent, speaks for itself. The CV here acts as a platform for your portfolio and lists achievements during your career.

Portfolio CVs are for senior managers, freelancers or those in creative fields and are often supported by a portfolio of work.

Most employers tend to prefer a two page CV (A4, single sided), but longer CVs are acceptable for specialist positions or where details of managed projects need to be relayed. Academic roles where publications are required to be listed may also require CVs of a longer length. One page CVs are useful for those without much of a career history and may focus more on educational or other related achievements.

Two page CVs are the most common in Britain. However, longer CVs can be used for project management and academic roles.

When it comes to CV layout it really is a personal choice, but there are plenty of templates out there for you to sample. Aside perhaps from creative CVs, remember to keep the format sober, professional and uncluttered. Put yourself in the reader's shoes – they are busy people and want to find the key information quickly without having to search for it. Help them out by telling them in an opening paragraph why you want the job and why you would be good for it.

CV templates are available online. Ensure that the format and layout is sober, professional and uncluttered. How easy is it for the recruiter to find the information they will want?

The body of the CV will typically consist of your past jobs, responsibilities and achievements. Don't be tempted to list everything you achieved in all your jobs; only mention your key responsibilities and list only the highlights your prospective employer will find

List only your key responsibilities and achievements that the recruiter will appreciate.

impressive and relevant. Here are some other general points to keep in mind:

- Keep your language concise, professional and jargon free.
- Avoid 'I/my' as in 'I/my revised procedures increased turnover by 75%'. Simply say 'revised procedures increased turnover by 75%'.
- Use the past tense for your career achievements and responsibilities but the present tense for your skills.
- Numbers hold tremendous power. Drop a few impressive statistics into your achievements in number form, ideally mentioning how much money was made or saved as a result if applicable.
- Avoid writing in capitals, apart from where essential (acronyms etc.).
- Show that you can take the initiative and achieve results. Rather than saying 'supervised the customer service team for retail operations', say 'co-ordinated and led the customer service team to improve satisfaction for retail operations by 29% in six months by harvesting best practices from unrelated industries'.

Avoid unprofessional language, rambling and jargon.

Avoid referring to yourself with 'I'.

Refer to your skills in the present tense but your responsibilities and career achievements in the past tense.

Use numbers to indicate successes – especially ones that result in money made or saved.

Avoid writing in capital letters where possible – this can indicate shouting.

Show that you can take the initiative and achieve results.

- Keep the typeface clear and professional. Use a 10-12 point font size in styles such as Times New Roman or Arial and space lines appropriately to avoid cluttering.

Use a clear font such as Times New Roman or Arial, point size 10-12 and space lines appropriately to avoid bunching.

Poor spelling and grammar will stick out to a recruiter. If you suspect that these may not be your strong points, ask a trusted friend to have a quick scan for you. There are also numerous CV agencies who will perform this service, as well as giving you further tips and advice.

Have your CV checked for spelling and grammar by a trusted friend or CV checking organisation.

Whilst a CV and covering letter alone won't get you a job, they will allow the employer to get a very good idea of who you are and what you may be able to do for them. Make yourself seem perfect for the job and you'll have a very good chance of getting an interview.

A covering letter should be an invitation for the recruiter to read your CV. It should instantly tell them you are the person for the job.

Finally, don't be tempted to lie on your CV. A good interviewer will question you about many aspects of it, and just one slip up can cause the whole ball of wool to unravel. Lying to get a job means you're trying to make yourself seem ready for something that you're not, and when you have trouble completing tasks your CV says you're a dab hand at, there will only be one result. Climbing the ladder step by step is less risky than jumping for a rung and missing.

Ethan's story

I joined a small engineering group from school and after my five year apprenticeship moved into development work and on to junior management. I had a young family to support, but when I was invited to join a newly established company with links to the group I jumped into the unknown.

I soon realised the new company was far from secure and required considerable work to make it profitable. I worked long hours, showed total commitment and was soon promoted to a Senior Manager, then invited to become a Director. They encouraged me to take a small stake in the company which meant parting with some of my hard earned cash but I saw it as a job for life and relished the deeper involvement. Luckily my mentor advised me not to spend the increasing salary, but to build up some security.

I didn't realise it at the time, but after ten years of success the tide had turned and we were in for three years of decline which would end for me in redundancy.

Rumours began to circulate about my fate and on a Friday morning I was asked to attend a meeting scheduled for later that day. This was not unusual but during the day I was tipped off by a colleague that I was to be made redundant. It was clear the decision had been taken without any consultation – it was only the formalities I was to attend for. I had some distance to travel to the meeting, which provided an opportunity to give an excuse for not attending, and instead received the redundancy letter on the following Monday.

I was devastated, 40 years old and after nearly 25 years of having a job I was unemployed. I was full of hatred and loathing for the person who I blamed for making this happen. This was a disaster. Everything I had worked for – my job, my status, my role in life – had been torn away from me. There followed a protracted period of wrangling over my leaving package but in the end I had a contract which had to be honoured. But it wasn't about the money – all I could think of was what I had lost and what was to be my future.

Fortunately I had heeded my mentor's advice to live within my means and for this I shall be forever grateful. I sat out the next five months occupied only with some home improvements and domestic chores. Then out of the blue a contact from the previous business set me up for a position working with disadvantaged members of society. It was a 9-5 job which I had not experienced for 20 years, but it refocused my life and returned my enthusiasm for management – allowing me to feel I was doing a worthwhile job, assisting others to make something of their life.

As a postscript the previous business continued to reduce in size and finally folded within five years.

"I've learned over the years that when somebody embellishes their resume... you don't hire them."

Dick Cheney

"CVs that demonstrated mindset at work and brought it to life just once were three times more likely than others to get the candidate an interview. Those that did it more than once were seven times more likely to get an interview." [6]

James Reed

"It's not hard to make decisions when you know what your values are."

Roy Disney

Step 9 – The interview process

Many of us find interviews extremely unpleasant, which is a situation often made worse if you haven't had an interview for a while. This section offers some advice for helping you through a successful interview and giving you the best chance of success, as well as outlining recent introductions and changes to the recruitment process.

Research the organisation

The internet has made this much easier to do, so you really have no excuse! A quick visit to the company website, especially the 'about us' section, will give you an overview of their aims, whilst a 'latest news' page should offer up-to-date information on their operations. It wouldn't hurt to jot a few items of the latest news down to repeat at the interview if the chance arises. This shows that you are interested in the company and their direction. A quick online search of the company's name could also throw up some important or interesting information not displayed on the website.

Presentation

As the saying goes, you don't get a second chance to make a first impression. Take the time and effort to turn out well groomed and in line with the culture of

Most of us find interviews unpleasant, especially if we haven't had one for a while.

The internet has made researching a company child's play – from their history to their last financial results.

Sharing some interesting information you found whilst researching will show an interest in the company – especially if they have a rich history.

Whilst companies may not necessarily have a dress code, it may be worth emulating how existing employees dress.

the organisation. If you're not sure of the 'dress code', preferably ask, or just look professional. Arrive five or ten minutes early and announce yourself at reception. You are likely to annoy your host if you arrive too early. Always phone with as much notice as possible if you expect to be delayed. If you can, visit the bathroom to check how you look and take some deep breaths to calm any nerves. Run through your key strengths to yourself whilst you do this. Remember that you are likely to be assessed from the moment you arrive. I recall reading a story in the newspaper recently of a person who went for an interview. After giving her details to the receptionist, she went to a quiet corner of the reception area, called her current employer and suddenly developed a terrible cough, stating that she would be unable to come into work. Needless to say, the receptionist at the potential new employer heard everything and passed the story on to the interviewer.

Back in reception; meet your interviewer with eye contact, a smile and a confident but not overpowering handshake. These may seem like small details, but a competent interviewer will notice if any are missing and will form an immediate impression of you. If you look good and appear confident you're off to a good start.

Arrive early to check you look your best and to calm any nerves. If you anticipate being late, phone as early as possible.

Meet your interviewer with a firm handshake, a smile and, crucially, eye contact. These small details don't go unnoticed.

Your job is to convince the interviewer that you tick all the boxes they require.

Know your CV inside out. Any glaring discrepancies will not look good.

Make an impact

Given the fact that you are being interviewed, someone within the company obviously thinks you have the potential to fulfil the role. Your job in the interview is to not only confirm this but, if possible, go beyond that. To start, know your CV inside out. Forgetting or mistaking roles, duties and dates of employment will make you look unprofessional and may lead the interviewer to query further areas of your CV for errors.

Have up your sleeve a couple of stories where you successfully negotiated similar incidents to those in the job you are interviewing for.

In an interview you are aiming to stand out from the competition, and there is no better way to do this than to show that you have already successfully performed some of the duties required of you in previous jobs. To this end, have some stories and specific examples up your sleeve where you have encountered and successfully remedied similar situations to those anticipated in the role, including any unforeseen benefits (profits, repeat business etc.).

Don't relay the entire Wikipedia entry for the company, but make sure you know a bit about the company's history, industry, aims and competitors.

The interviewer won't expect you to know the entire company history, number of staff in the building and the financial projections for the next quarter, but showing that you have researched a little of their history, their aims, what they do and who their competition is will show you are interested in the company as a whole and not just the job. Don't

Keep your answers concise and to the point without appearing short. Rambling through answers and avoiding the question won't instil your interviewer with confidence.

bamboozle them with facts and figures though, and only provide them when appropriate.

Finally, it never hurts to bring a couple of props to show off your work. This can include a handbook for a project you worked on, a training manual you put together – anything in fact that relates to the job you're interviewing for that will make a positive impression.

Less is more

Try to keep your answers as concise and to the point as possible, but without coming across as curt. How you answer the question reflects how you work and you want the interviewer to see you as someone who gets the job done thoroughly, professionally and with a minimum of fuss. Over talking, especially off the topic in hand, displays a lack of focus and a possible tendency to mentally wander. Structured answers without waffling work best.

Nerves

Interviewers will expect you to be at least a little bit nervous, but over anxiety can represent a concern to them – as can over confidence. A reasonable interviewer however will always cut you some slack as far as nerves go. If you find the nerves taking over (heart thumping, shaking, sweating) you can always ask

If appropriate, bring in props such as a handbook or portfolio of a project you worked on or a training manual you put together – anything relevant to the job that will help sell you.

All interviewers anticipate nerves, but try to avoid over anxiety.

If you start to feel overly nervous, ask for a glass of water if one isn't offered, take deep breaths before giving your answers and concentrate on delivering your responses.

Maintain eye contact without staring and don't forget to smile.

for a glass of water. Take a deep breath before each answer (pass it off as careful consideration) and focus on talking slowly, pronouncing each word and taking regular small breaths where needed to avoid gabbling entire sentences. Ensure you maintain eye contact as much as possible, but without staring. A smile now and again doesn't hurt either. If in any doubt, try mirroring the expressions and actions of your interviewer. This is a known method of helping someone to relate to you.

Questions

Many people overlook the power of asking questions. Searching, but relevant questions will show that you have researched the position, the company and the market in which it operates. Researching the company will more often than not throw up some questions which, combined with anything you want to know about your own position and opportunities, will show that you are interested about wider aspects of the company than just your welfare.

Searching, but relevant questions from you to the interviewer will reinforce your interest in the role and your research into the company.

As well as traditional face-to-face interviews, other forms of assessment are used which are worth mentioning (you may be exposed to a combination of them through one recruitment process):

Assessment centres involve spending time with other candidates completing team oriented and role-playing tasks and interviews.

Other forms of interview often take place in contemporary recruitment processes.

Assessment centres will involve you spending some time with other candidates going through a series of assessments such as interviews, case studies, group and role-playing exercises. These test your teamwork, analytical and leadership skills and feel more relaxed than standard interviews, although you will be monitored throughout.

Psychometric tests are usually written but sometimes verbal tests that offer employers an insight into your characteristics and methods of working. They often include aptitude (verbal, numerical, abstract, spatial, mechanical) and personality analysis questionnaires, usually with a mixture of free response (your own words), multiple choice (several options) or forced choice (two options) answers. There are inexpensive yet valuable books available to help you prepare for psychometric tests.

In performance based tests you are assessed on how well or quickly you can perform certain tasks. They include tests of attainment (maths, spelling or typing tests or tests of specialist knowledge), ability (verbal, numerical or special tests) and aptitude (how quickly you can pick up new skills).

Whatever test or interview you undertake, try to make sure that you leave the interviewer with the impression that you are professional, keen and dedicated, and that you haven't let your redundancy affect you. You know you are the right person for the job – all you have to do is let them know.

Psychometric tests offer employers insights into your characteristics and ways of working. They employ a variety of questionnaires and tests to reveal thought patterns.

Performance based tests examine how well and quickly you perform certain mental and physical tasks.

Whatever your method of assessment, try to ensure that the employer leaves with a positive view of you and that you do what you can to stand out from the crowd.

Clive Lewis

Raymond's story

I have never been much of an aspirational man; all I need to make me happy is a job and enough money to look after my family. To this end I rarely went seeking promotions, preferring security and stability over power. I had been a Supervisor at the depot of a national logistics firm for seven years, having started work on the shop floor. I liked the firm, the location and the security, and while it would never make me a millionaire, I was happy enough. A couple of security problems in depots abroad caused the company to lose business, and before I knew it I was reading about buyouts in the press. I was naturally concerned about my position and asked my boss for reassurance about my role – reassurance he couldn't give me. I was now terrified of losing my job, not only because of the affect on me, but also my family. My wife had been a housewife for about 15 years and would have had difficulty looking for work with the income we needed, leaving me as the main breadwinner. Given my relatively limited skill set I too was worried I would face a difficult time looking for work again, not to mention the blow to my pride.

Almost inevitably I was one of those selected for redundancy when the takeover was completed. I was gutted and embarrassed; I was supposed to be the head of my family and I couldn't even keep a job. I'm not one for revealing my emotions so I braved it out in front of my family, which was possibly one of the worst things I could have done. A few drinks with a close friend who also got made redundant at the same time was the breaking point – we were both almost in tears over it together! We ended up helping and supporting each other, looking in the papers for jobs and speaking to other people we knew in the same industry. A friend of mine who worked in HR helped me with my CV and covering letter and advised me how to go about targeting firms and applying for jobs. He was a godsend! I must have applied for almost every job in the paper and online, a large number of which I was totally unsuitable for and, on reflection, am glad I didn't get!

Eventually a close friend who knew that I had previously dabbled in pottery offered me what was effectively an apprenticeship at his company – he made pots, vases and the like for garden centres and had a couple of new contracts he needed help with. The pay was low but the thought of working with a friend doing something I would definitely enjoy, swung it for me. I was still unsure after a few weeks, but before I knew it, we were having a great time and I found myself doing something I loved and with a good friend to boot. I was gradually given more responsibility and moved into an administration role as another couple of contracts came in. It didn't take long for my new earnings to eclipse those of my old job, and I am now in charge of one of the major contracts, dealing with clients as well as assisting in the manufacture of the items when I get a chance. Whilst the lack of redundancy would obviously have been less stressful for all concerned, on the flip side I would never have got the opportunity to progress as I did. Reflecting on life and taking a chance really did work out, and I would advise anyone in a similar position to do the same, as long as the odds aren't too much against you!

"Concentration is a fine antidote to anxiety."

Jack Nicklaus

"So many people out there have no idea what they want to do for a living, but they think that by going on job interviews they'll magically figure it out. If you're not sure, that message comes out loud and clear in the interview."

Todd Bermont

"Not knowing enough about the company or position, displaying a bad attitude or inquiring about compensation prematurely can all leave a negative impression with hiring managers."

Max Messmer

Step 10 – Lifelong learning & skills

With the changes we are experiencing in the job market there has never been a better time to focus on lifelong learning. The desire and drive to constantly evolve one's learning is a key to continued success – companies such as Google, Apple and Gillette are always looking for new avenues to explore and new technologies to exploit. Missed opportunities can cost billions.

Learning should never stop. The most successful companies are those that continue to search for new avenues and learn about new technologies.

Lifelong learning is just as important for individuals; those who stop learning and exploring new opportunities limit the directions that life can take them. I once spoke on this topic at a conference for education professionals, and in preparing my speech I thought of my own previous learning and classroom exercises that looked at various PEST models. PEST normally stands for Political, Economic, Social and Technical, but with a few amendments to the original model here is a PEST framework that supports lifelong learning.

When we stop learning ourselves we limit the directions in which life can take us.

Personal benefits – learning brings confidence and growth, allowing us to actively engage on a variety of topics.

Personal – Learning brings personal confidence and growth. Absorbing new information and facts and maintaining awareness of developments in these areas allows us to be better able to engage in dialogue and put our opinions across on a wider variety of topics. This also has the added benefit of making us seem, rightly or not, to be more intelligent, and thus become more respected – someone people go to on certain matters.

Economic – Across the developed world, and the political spectrum, everybody agrees about the importance of education. It is good for society, which needs the contributions and economic productivity – not to mention the tax – of a skilled workforce, and it is good for individuals. People with a higher standard of education earn more, are more satisfied with their work and leisure time, are less likely to be unemployed, unhealthy or take part in criminal activity, and are more likely to volunteer their time and vote in elections. According to the US Department of Labor, a student who went to high school but didn't graduate with a diploma earned an average of $419 per week. This sum rose to $595 for those who had graduated with a diploma, $1,039 for those who had gone on to college and earned a bachelor's degree, and $1,200 for those with an advanced degree[7].

Social – When people are engaged in learning, there is a high likelihood that dependency on organisations such as Social Services will reduce or be completely eliminated, which is of huge benefit to the country in a variety of ways. A more educated society also leads to a more cordial, responsible and understanding society.

Economic benefits – learning and education benefits the economy in a number of ways, from taxation on higher salaries to raised revenue from improved business.

Social benefits – a more educated society is often a more cordial and responsible society. Reliance on state handouts is also reduced.

Tactical – Continued learning can help put the building blocks in place to move from one role to another. If you have identified an area of work that you would like to engage in but are not quite ready for, learning can help bridge the gap to get you to the role you have your eye on.

Tactical benefits – further learning can bridge gaps in knowledge to allow you to move from one job to another or progress in an existing role.

Lifelong learning can therefore enrich our lives both professionally and personally. Learning about other cultures for example can make us more informed when it comes to dealing with foreign clients or customers, whilst learning a foreign language is known to increase employment options. Continual learning is also an important feature of later life; regular mental stimulation keeps the brain active and can, according to research, aid memory and help stave off illnesses such as Dementia and Alzheimer's.

Continual learning can enrich our lives both professionally and socially. Learning a foreign language for example can both widen our scope for potential employment and open up new social avenues.

There are countless ways in which continual learning will help you grow, both professionally and personally. Whichever way you choose to do it, prospective employers will be impressed that you have used the time and money from your redundancy to educate yourself in new areas. It will show not only that you are willing to evolve your education and can do so quickly and effectively, but also that you can adapt to different environments in a positive manner. In the same way that banks look more favourably on those who have taken out and repaid loans than those who have never

Employers will be impressed that you have used your redundancy time and money to widen your learning – make sure you mention it.

borrowed in their lives, some employers will favour candidates who have triumphed over adversity than those who have never faced it.

Lindsey's story

The first time I was made redundant I thought my world was going to end. My first career was ended after ten years' hard work by a combination of de-privatisation and an embittered, hostile manager. 30 years on I can still remember the shock and the tears at realising that my dreams had ended prematurely and that I would no longer see the people who were more friends than colleagues. The first lesson I learned here was that if there is money on the table, and there should be, take it – but negotiate hard. I realised too that there was no point in trying to reverse a decision that had already been made.

This experience was followed seven years later by another redundancy. The emotional wrench was even worse this time, added to the fact that this was from a better job with better pay. Whilst trying to recover from this second setback someone gave me some great advice. He told me to draw nine boxes and divide my life into important areas as I saw them (family, hobbies, health, money etc.). I only ended up with one box – work. This presented an obvious problem that I needed to deal with. I managed to find myself a more challenging job and set about creating more boxes, but it was not long lived – the recession hit and I was, once again, without work. Following this I found another position, but learnt another lesson – don't take a big money, high pressure job just to show someone (or yourself) you can be a success.

Finally, after three redundancies, I am five years into a complete career change, with all nine boxes full. I used my redundancy money wisely and invested in property, with the result that I am now in charge of a million pound property portfolio and I work with a great team. Sadly I don't have the same 'can't wait to get to work' feeling that I used to have, but this is partly because I have purposefully kept a little more of an

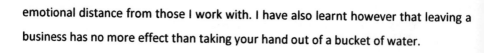

emotional distance from those I work with. I have also learnt however that leaving a business has no more effect than taking your hand out of a bucket of water.

"Our progress as a nation can be no swifter than our progress in education."

John F. Kennedy

"Get over the idea that only children should spend their time in study. Be a student so long as you still have something to learn, and this will mean all your life."

Henry L. Doherty

"I don't think much of a man who is not wiser today than he was yesterday."

Abraham Lincoln

Step 11 – Mindset

In a world of qualifications, training and transferable skills, it is sometimes easy to forget what employers really want. According to a recent survey by national recruitment consultancy firm Reed, 96% of the 1,263 organisations questioned said they would rather hire someone without the complete skill set but with the right mindset over the alternative[8]. So if skills alone won't get you the job, what will? What is it that employers are looking for?

It's not just skills that employers want – they want to know that you have the drive and desire to do the job too.

The answer is 'values' – the core traits that come together to make up an individual's attitude to their work. Employers are looking for candidates with the right skill set *and* the right mindset – in other words they want someone with the tools to do the job and drive to get it done on time and professionally. So what are these values and how can you show them off?

Many employers hold these character traits, or values, in higher esteem than an employee's skill set, including 96% of over 1,000 organisations recently surveyed.

Most importantly to employers is a **strong work ethic**. This doesn't just mean working hard, it also means working smart. Prospective employers will want to see that you have the drive to see tasks through to the end, that you take pride in what you do and that you work intelligently and within constraints of time and money. Try to think of examples when you have shown dedication towards a task above and beyond what was expected of you.

Employers will want to be sure that you have a strong work ethic. This means not just that you work hard but that you work smart too. Try to think of examples that display both.

Bouncing Back From Redundancy

Linked to work ethic is **teamwork** – an essential value in almost any workplace, in any industry. Individuals who can demonstrate that they are team players, that they are prepared to offer support, receive advice and work with their team to achieve common goals, will be highly regarded. It may be a cliché to say that you are a team player, but it is an important one to remember and demonstrate.

Teamwork is also a crucial value for the modern day worker to possess. Recalling an experience where teamwork helped solve a problem or complete a difficult task will demonstrate your abilities in this area.

Employers will also want to be sure of your **dependability and responsibility**. They will want to know that you will be somewhere when you say you'll be there and that you won't shirk from the responsibility of your position when things get difficult or if you fall behind schedule. This relates back to basic issues of trust, the foundations on which all relationships are built. Try and demonstrate instances where you were in a position of trust and responsibility, ideally ones in which you volunteered your efforts.

Employers will need to know that you are dependable and reliable. They will want to know that you can be trusted to carry out your duties honestly and to the best of your ability, but that you will ask for help if you need it.

Those with a **positive attitude** are also favoured by employers, perhaps for obvious reasons; someone with a positive attitude will approach a problem and see how it can be overcome, whereas someone with a negative attitude might let the first setback be the last. Try to demonstrate instances when you have overcome a series of issues on the way to successfully tackling a problem.

Employers like positive attitudes. Make sure that when you approach potential employers you are keen, enthusiastic and confident about taking on challenges.

Professionalism is also a key value employers look for. Professionals look, dress and speak in a manner reflecting their profession, company and personal pride. Clients and customers expect to be dealt with in a professional manner, so make sure you treat potential employers in the way you would treat clients and customers.

Other values to consider putting across to prospective employers include adaptability, self-motivation, self-confidence, desire for personal growth and loyalty. Be careful not to reel off this entire list of values in an interview. Instead, drop them into the conversation as appropriate and always try to back them up with examples if you can. Hopefully a combination of directly relevant skills and a broad base of core values will make you the perfect candidate.

Employers also demand professionalism. They want to know that you will be a good ambassador for the company. Make sure the way you look, dress and act match the requirements of the company.

Also consider mentioning your adaptability, self-motivation, self-confidence, desire for personal growth and loyalty – but not all at the same time. Drop them into conversation where relevant.

Samantha's story

I was made redundant after two and a half years with an organisation. My line manager, with whom I had clashed, called me into his office and informed me very matter of factly that my job was at risk. He told me not to discuss the nature of the conversation with any of my colleagues. Nothing more was said until around ten days later when I emailed him and asked for an update. He then phoned and said that he met with the CEO the week before, and it had been decided that my post was likely to be made redundant. This was confirmed at a meeting later that week where I was told that I would be leaving the company within two months. At this stage the consultation process had not even been formalised, but already he had asked a colleague to prepare rough redundancy figures which I was given at the meeting.

Later that week I was told that a consultation process would commence the following Monday, giving me only two days to prepare and source a representative. As I was not in a union and my line manager had expressly told me not to discuss my redundancy with work colleagues, this was particularly difficult. Eventually I had to discreetly ask colleagues in other teams in order to try and find someone who would be willing to support me. As I had been experiencing bullying from my manager, I doubted from the outset that this was a genuine redundancy. His aggressive and domineering behaviour towards me had become so obvious that immediate colleagues and staff members in other teams would often comment. There were issues and arguments leading up to the meeting, to the point where I felt like my manager wanted me to walk away without a redundancy package or even a reference. Eventually the redundancy consultation continued, with my manager and I rarely engaging in conversation outside of it.

It has been three months since I left that company and I am undertaking some interim work. The first month was difficult as I spent a lot of time 'coming down' from such an awful experience. The cards and gifts I received from my colleagues still remain unopened. I had spent a lot of time feeling quite low, not because of being made redundant (I have experienced redundancy on two previous occasions) but more because of the manner in which I was singled out by my manager. Finding another full time job has proved more difficult than I imagined it would be. I was at first quite fanatical in trying to find a comparable position to the job I had been made redundant from, but now having had time to reflect I realise that it is no longer that important.

Initially I was really disappointed with myself and felt like I was a failure, then one day I had a moment of clarity. Prior to my redundancy, my salary was the most I had ever earned. It was also the hardest I had ever worked and the most fearful and unsafe I had ever felt in any working environment. I may only be earning half of what I was in my previous role, but I no longer work long hours in the office, I no longer bring work home and I no longer have the constant worry of facing a bullying and unsupportive manager every day. The stress I was experiencing has all but disappeared and I generally feel calmer and able to sleep properly. Other than the minor niggling worries about settling back into secure employment, I generally feel much happier. I have had time to sit and reflect about my experience and where I will go from here. I no longer have any desire to return to the field of finance but instead will be focusing on a new direction. I started studying law prior to being made redundant and am now actively pursuing a career where I can develop in this area. My confidence had taken a real tumble but I feel that I am turning a corner and I'm getting things back on track. I have had the opportunity to explore different opportunities because I am no longer constrained by the perceived security of a permanent position. I now view the redundancy as a positive outcome. I couldn't have carried on in that environment and I feel that life is already better as a consequence.

"It is a thousand times better to have common sense without education than to have education without common sense."

Robert G. Ingersoll

"Be careful how you think. Your life is shaped by your thoughts."

Proverbs 4 v 23

"If you aren't fired with enthusiasm, you will be fired with enthusiasm."

Vince Lombardi

Step 12 – Letting go

Whilst successfully finding a job after redundancy should eliminate external concerns such as financial and career worries, psychological concerns may linger for some time afterwards. This is completely normal and is nothing to be worried about in the short term. Redundancy can be a traumatic time, and those wounds don't just heal if you find a new job. Instead, many people find themselves feeling a raft of ongoing emotions, which we will look at in this section.

A new job doesn't always eliminate the psychological effects of redundancy, but it will certainly help.

Many who experience redundancy find themselves experiencing continuing feelings of **anger** towards their former employer, even after starting a new job. This is perfectly understandable, but such emotions can affect one's health if left to fester. Individuals who feel anger in this manner tend to deal with it in one of three ways; by expressing it, by pushing it away or by calming down naturally. Expressing it, either in diary/journal form or through conversation, is a healthy form of release, as is working out your anger through sport or other exercise. Suppressing the anger will only prolong the negative feelings and could see them translated into negative behaviour, which is obviously something to be avoided. Some find their anger dissipating once their lot improves, and letting nature take its course in this manner is the best possible outcome. If you feel

You may find that feelings of anger towards your former company or individuals within that company don't subside.

Try expressing your anger through journaling or talking with someone or channel your efforts into your new job or career. Focus and allow time to heal the wounds. Avoid suppressing the anger.

you have real problems finding ways to let go of your anger, it may be an idea to speak to your GP or arrange some private counselling.

Your redundancy may have also left you with a feeling of **fragility** – that something terrible could go wrong at any moment. Like anger, these feelings can spread to other avenues of your life if not reversed. Proving yourself in your new role and receiving praise for what you do will certainly help overcome these fears. Time spent establishing yourself in your new role, or even gaining a promotion, will greatly reduce these fears and will bring some stability back into your life. Throwing yourself into your new role and enjoying its fruits, maybe with a new hobby or activity, will help focus your mind on the right things and will quickly re-establish your sense of self-worth and will begin restoring your confidence in your own abilities.

Alternatively, some people feel more **motivated** to succeed than ever before following redundancy. There are many stories of those who started up businesses in direct competition to those from which they were made redundant and eventually overtook them. The ability to use such a setback as a motivational tool is one that many would pay good money for. Self-employment is often the avenue chosen by these individuals because of the potential sense of achievement in success.

You may be feeling more fragile following your redundancy, that something else might go wrong at any time. These feelings should fade over time as security and routine return to your life.

Using your free time to try new pursuits or hobbies helps to focus the mind and achieve the success and confidence you may feel you need.

Some people use redundancy as a motivational tool for succeeding, often in a position of self-employment.

Finally, it is worth bearing in mind that, strange as it may sound, the person who made you redundant might be suffering as much as you, or worse. A study by AHIM[9] found that 44% of 200 managers interviewed were involved in redundancy programmes but had received no prior training, with 38% experiencing a detrimental health and family life as a result. 71% of managers who were expected to be asked to undergo redundancy programmes also believed that they would be stressed and upset if they had to make people redundant. It is clear therefore that redundancy has wide reaching consequences on both sides of the redundancy issue.

As I have discussed throughout this book, positive thinking is the key to overcoming redundancy at every stage in the process. Those who can see their redundancy as a past event that has no relation to their current or future worth will recover quicker and will ultimately enjoy a more satisfactory working life. Moving on from redundancy will be easier for some than for others, but you will eventually rebuild yourself and as a result you will be a stronger person for the experience.

Research has shown that managers involved in issuing redundancy notices also suffer as a result of the process, sometimes more than the employee made redundant.

Positive thinking is vital to getting over redundancy. Seeing it as a past event and treating your job search as just that will help you forget about it, as will forcing yourself to make positive steps. The results of which should begin to help you recover and look forward.

My story

After leaving school at 16 I began working for a large retailer, starting on the shop floor and working my way up to Branch Manager. After this I signed up to five years of part time study at university, leaving the company in order to find a HR role that fitted my new qualifications. For the next eight years or so I had a magnificent time building my career. I got promoted, secured bigger and more exciting jobs and even started to fly around the world, now as a HR Director.

Out of the blue one day I was called to my CEO's office. The organisation had decided to dispose of some subsidiary companies and there would be no need for a Group HR Director, which was my role. I was the first of 50 people that were about to be given a similar message. My boss told me first as the company wanted my help to manage the transition. The real truth of the matter however was that he wanted to test my frame of mind upon hearing the message. Even though I wasn't totally taken by surprise, when the message came I still went into shock. The next six months were spent managing the redundancy process for my colleagues whilst dealing with my own redundancy at the same time – a very strange experience.

My redundancy experience prompted me to think about other aspects of my life. Even though I had worked in some really exciting roles, including being a HR Director of a FTSE250 company, I realised that I wasn't totally fulfilled. The result of this thought process was that I became heavily involved in charity work, helping people from poor socio-economic backgrounds. It was during the redundancy period that I also started to plan the route to starting my own business, specialising in dispute resolution and HR consulting. I continue to be heavily involved in charity work and have founded a couple of charities. Recently, my work in both fields was recognised by being awarded an OBE for Public Service in the 2011 Queen's Birthday Honours List. If I had never experienced redundancy, it is highly unlikely that I would have set out on this career trajectory and that I would have been awarded a national honour for my work.

"Celebrate endings – for they precede new beginnings."

Jonathan Lockwood Huie

"Life is not about waiting for the storms to pass. It's about learning how to dance in the rain."

Vivian Greene

"How do geese know when to fly to the sun? Who tells them the seasons? How do we, humans know when it is time to move on? As with the migrant birds, so surely with us, there is a voice within if only we would listen to it, that tells us certainly when to go forth into the unknown."

Elisabeth Kubler-Ross

Conclusion

The aim of this handbook has been to help you deal with your redundancy and provide you with an idea of what steps to take in order to minimise its effects and get back to work as quickly as possible. I myself know how it feels to be made redundant, but I recovered and, like many others, have my redundancy to thank for giving me the chance to be more successful than I would have been had I not lost that job.

The real life case studies throughout this handbook are littered with examples of stories of people who have bounced back from their redundancy experience and have gone on to bigger and better things. In some cases, people are now working in roles to which they are more suited. In others, people are enjoying a better quality of life. There are also other well documented examples of people who have changed their life beyond recognition following redundancy. For example, Will King, founder of King of Shaves, was made redundant two years before starting his company which now boasts revenues in excess of £25m. Debbie Davis was made redundant from a printing firm in 2004 and struggled to pay rent until she started working as an Avon representative. In 2010 she made the news because of her £250k annual earning from the job. As you can see, redundancy can take you places you may never have dreamed of! These latter examples are unlikely to be run of the mill, and of course, money isn't everything. Nevertheless, they are part of a collection of stories that demonstrate that all isn't necessarily lost when you hear the news that you are to be made redundant.

A redundancy plan like the one in this book is a little like a domestic fire evacuation plan – ideally we should all have one, but the reality is that many of us don't think anything that bad will happen to us. As you have probably discovered however, redundancy can happen – and by reading this book you have taken the first in a number of important positive steps towards making it work for you. Using your redundancy rather than suffering from it requires the right mindset from the very start, but dealing with it in the ways I have outlined should help you avoid the pitfalls that trap many. Adopting the practices and techniques in this book will give you a definite advantage over those who do no research and those who panic, which is a great many, and will hopefully get you back to work in no time. Good luck!

References

1. http://www.lewisalexander.com/blog/2011/03/over-1500-people-being-made-redundant-every-day/

2. http://www.itpro.co.uk/609647/it-staff-brace-themselves-for-redundancy

3. Claire Macaulay, "Job Mobility and Job Tenure in the UK", 2003

4. Paul Gregg and Jonathan Wadsworth, "The Labour Market in Winter: The State of Working Britain", 2011

5. http://www.change-management-coach.com/kübler-ross.html

6. James Reed and Paul G Stoltz, "Put Your Mindset to Work: The One Asset You Really Need to Win and Keep the Job You Love", 2011

7. Bureau of Labor Statistics, Weekly and Hourly Earnings Data from the Current Population Survey. Washington, DC: US Department of Labor, 2007

8. James Reed and Paul G Stoltz, "Put Your Mindset to Work: The One Asset You Really Need to Win and Keep the Job You Love", 2011

9. http://www.management-issues.com/display_page.asp?section=research&id=2922

Bouncing Back From Redundancy training course

A training course is available for those wanting to explore career options as a result of redundancy, change or other significant event. The course encompasses the 12 steps covered in this handbook and equips delegates with everything they need to know about making the right career choice. It is also ideal as part of a package for organisations offering outplacement support.

The course will allow you to:

- Manage your career effectively

- Find out more about your personal strengths and weaknesses

- Discover the secrets behind finding jobs in the hidden market

- Hone your interview skills and techniques

- Improve your chances of reducing your time out of work

Globis Mediation Group has nearly 10 years' experience in improving employee and company performance. All courses are run by experienced specialists, so you can be sure that a Globis training course will provide you with the very best training and advice. For more information on this or any of our other courses, or to book online, visit www.globis.co.uk.

Other Books by Clive Lewis OBE

The Definitive Guide to Workplace Mediation & Managing Conflict at Work

This book is ideal for those seeking to learn more about the concept of mediation in the workplace and the time and money that can be saved by engaging conflict resolution strategies.

Win Win: Resolving Workplace Conflict: 12 Stories

This book presents a series of 12 stories that bring to life tales of difficulty and the role played by the author as a mediator and dispute resolution specialist. This book will be of benefit to anyone dealing with workplace conflict.

Difficult Conversations – 10 Steps to Becoming a Tackler not a Dodger

In life you are either a tackler or a dodger. This easy read book provides you with 10 simple steps to boost your skills and confidence allowing you to tackle, not dodge that difficult conversation.

Order form

Bouncing Back From Redundancy
12 Steps to Get Your Career and Life Back on Track

Book Quantity	Price
1-14 copies	£9.99 each
15-29 copies	£7.99 each
30-99 copies	£5.99 each
100-999 copies	£5.75 each
1,000-4,999 copies	£5.50 each
5,000-9,999 copies	£5.25 each
10,000 or more copies	£5.00 each
eBooks – per book	Price
	£6.99

Name: .... Job Title: ....

Organisation: ....

Address: ....

Postcode: .... Tel No: ....

Email: ....

(Postage and packing £3 – please contact Globis for multiple or overseas purchases)
☐ Cheque enclosed (Please make payable to Globis Ltd)
☐ Please invoice *(only if over £100)*
☐ Please debit my credit card

Name on Card: .... Card Number: ....

Start Date: .... Expiry Date: .... Security No: ....

Signed: ....

Post completed form to: Globis Ltd, Unit 1, Wheatstone Court, Quedgeley, Gloucester GL2 2AQ

Tel:	0330 100 0809
Fax:	01452 726001
Email:	info@globis.co.uk

About the author

Clive Lewis OBE is a leading employee relations and dispute resolution specialist, facilitator, coach, trainer, author and speaker. He is founding director of the Globis Mediation Group, and an accredited commercial mediator specialising in helping to solve complex one on one, team, organisational, multiparty and collective disputes. His work covers the private, public and third sectors and he has mediated hundreds of disputes. He is the author of four books including 'The Definitive Guide to Workplace Mediation', 'Win Win: Resolving Workplace Conflict: 12 Stories' and 'Difficult Conversations – 10 Steps to Becoming a Tackler not a Dodger' as well as numerous published articles on mediation in the workplace. He serves as Honorary Secretary on the board of the Civil Mediation Council, a council which acts as an advisory organisation to government on issues relating to the progression of mediation in England and Wales, and chairs the council's workplace committee. His work has taken him across three continents and has included advising governments outside the UK.

In addition to his day job, he is a non-executive director in the NHS, a Trustee of the National Youth Jazz Orchestra and another small charity, and Chair of the Open College Network. His commitment to charity work led to him being appointed as Chair of a government appointed independent panel exploring the rising costs of youth underachievement, of which four of the five recommendations put forward were accepted. He is currently studying towards completing a PhD. In 2011 he was awarded an OBE for public service.

Step 3 Exercise sheet

My skills	What I don't enjoy
e.g. Creating spreadsheets	e.g. Public speaking
Advanced user of Excel and Access	Presenting
Writing and proofreading	Accounts

Notes

Notes